Sustainable Innovation: A Comprehensive Guide for a Regenerative Future

Preface

Welcome to "Sustainable Innovation: A Comprehensive Guide for a Regenerative Future." In an era where the urgency of sustainability becomes increasingly evident, this book aims to be a compass for navigating the complex world of sustainable innovation.

We live in a time of extraordinary opportunities and unprecedented challenges, where innovation is not just an option but a necessity. This comprehensive guide is crafted with the belief that through innovation, we can shape a regenerative future, where human progress harmoniously aligns with respect for our planet.

From clear definitions of sustainable innovation to practical examples of companies and communities leading the way, each chapter is designed to provide an in-depth understanding of the challenges and opportunities that lie ahead. Together, we will explore the foundations of sustainability, analyze the current state of environmental practices, and discuss how innovation can be the driving force towards sustainable solutions.

Success stories from businesses, communities, and individuals demonstrate that creating a positive impact is possible. From emerging technologies to grassroots initiatives, this book is an invitation to explore, learn, and take action. We conclude our journey with a vision of a sustainable and resilient future, fueled by education, awareness, and global collaboration. Whether you are a industry professional, a curious student, or a citizen eager to contribute to change, this guide is tailored for you. We are all involved in this mission of transformation, and our collective commitment can make a difference.

Consider this guide as a resource to inform, inspire, and, most importantly, to take concrete actions. The sustainable future we envision is within our reach, and every step matters. We are excited to share this journey with you and to be part of a global community dedicated to creating a better world for present and future generations.
Safe travels towards a regenerative future!

Chapter 1: Introduction to Sustainable Innovation

In the vast landscape of technological growth and economic development, sustainable innovation emerges as the keystone to shape a resilient future in harmony with the environment and society. This chapter inaugurates our journey into the fascinating world of sustainable innovation, exploring the foundations of this discipline and laying the groundwork for a profound and conscious reflection on our relationship with the planet.

Definition of Sustainable Innovation

Sustainable innovation is not merely a concept but an ethical and pragmatic imperative. It refers to the ability to develop creative and advanced solutions that meet present needs without compromising the ability of future generations to meet their own. It is a dynamic process that integrates economic efficiency, social equity, and environmental responsibility. In other words, sustainable innovation is the engine propelling us to rethink our relationship with the world, steering us towards a future where prosperity is built upon a harmonious balance between humanity and the environment.

Current Context and the Importance of Sustainability

We live in a crucial era where our actions directly impact the planet. Climate change, biodiversity loss, and the depletion of natural resources are unequivocal signs that our current trajectory is unsustainable. Sustainable innovation represents the crucial response to this global challenge, emerging as a beacon of hope in the darkness of the environmental crisis. The adoption of innovative solutions aims not only to reduce the negative impact of our activities but also to create a future where economic growth intertwines with environmental conservation and social inclusion.

Objectives of the Book and Structure of Subsequent Chapters

This book is an enlightening journey through the world of sustainable innovation, designed to inspire, inform, and guide the reader on a path of discovery. Through a comprehensive approach, we will delve into the foundations of sustainability, analyze the current state of environmental challenges, explore the crucial role of innovation, and immerse ourselves in key sectors such as design thinking, sustainable industry, green technologies, and sustainable mobility.

Our goal is to provide a complete and in-depth overview of sustainable innovation, offering a clear framework of the opportunities and challenges that lie ahead. Through reading this book, we hope readers gain a thorough understanding of the need to adopt sustainable practices and feel motivated to contribute to positive change. Embarking on this journey together, we are aware that only through sustainable innovation can we hope to shape a future where prosperity is shared by all, and our common home, planet Earth, is preserved for future generations. Welcome to a world of enlightening ideas and solutions that guide us towards a sustainable path for tomorrow.

Chapter 2: Foundations of Sustainability

In the intricate fabric of sustainability, fundamental principles intertwine to delineate the path towards a harmonious and enduring world. This chapter is a deep journey into the foundations of sustainability, exploring key principles that are the lifeblood of any initiative aimed at preserving our planet and building a fair future for all.

Key Principles of Sustainability

The cornerstone principles of sustainability are reflected in a holistic vision where every action and decision is weighed considering the impact on social, environmental, and economic aspects. The adoption of sustainable practices implies careful consideration of the interconnections between the elements of our world. Resource conservation, promotion of equity, and respect for the environment thus become the cornerstones of a sustainable path. Through the implementation of these principles, there is an effort to redefine the very concept of progress, shifting focus from blind growth to shared prosperity that embraces both present and future generations.

Triple Bottom Line: People, Planet, Profit

A central pillar of sustainability is the concept of the "Triple Bottom Line," an approach that goes beyond the traditional financial assessment of economic activities. This revolutionary model, proposed by John Elkington, introduces three "P"s: People, Planet, Profit.
People: Social equity is a cornerstone of sustainability. It means ensuring that economic and social decisions take into

account existing disparities, promoting universal access to resources, and the benefits of economic growth. In a sustainable context, every individual should enjoy equal opportunities and living conditions.

Planet: Environmental sustainability is crucial to preserving biodiversity, protecting ecosystems, and reducing the negative impact of human activities. The adoption of practices that promote energy efficiency, responsible resource use, and climate change mitigation is fundamental to ensuring a healthy and prosperous planet.

Profit: Profit, in the context of sustainability, is not merely financial but represents a global value. It is about creating long-term value, balancing economic prosperity with social well-being and environmental protection. A sustainable approach to profit involves a reduced ecological footprint and a positive social impact.

The Importance of Social, Environmental, and Economic Equity

Equity is the glue that holds together the principles of sustainability. Social equity involves ensuring that every individual has access to the same opportunities, regardless of socioeconomic background, ethnicity, or gender. Environmental equity emphasizes the fair distribution of environmental benefits and burdens, ensuring that vulnerable communities are not disproportionately affected by negative impacts such as pollution. Economic equity aims to reduce economic inequalities, promoting a more equitable distribution of wealth.
This chapter is an invitation to delve into the intrinsic principles of sustainability, paving the way

for a deeper understanding of how we can collectively shape a future where equity and sustainability intertwine to create a resilient and shared narrative.

Chapter 3: Current State of Sustainability

In this chapter, we delve deeply into the current reality of sustainability, examining the global environmental challenges that confront our common home, Earth. Through acute analysis, we explore the impacts of our actions on the environment and confront the imperative need for radical change, oriented towards the adoption of sustainable practices.

Analysis of Global Environmental Challenges

Our planet is in balance, and the list of global environmental challenges is long and complex. From climate change to biodiversity loss, from deforestation to air and water pollution, every aspect of our environment is threatened. Environmental challenges know no borders; they are

interconnected and require a global approach to be effectively addressed.
The rise in temperatures, primarily caused by greenhouse gas emissions, is triggering extreme climate events, initiating a cycle of changes that jeopardize food security, human health, and ecosystem stability. The accelerated loss of biodiversity threatens the resilience of ecosystems, depriving us of vital resources and disrupting delicate balances that support life on Earth.

Impacts of Human Actions on the Environment

Human actions have been the primary driver of these environmental challenges. Industrialization, intensive exploitation of natural resources, and large-scale waste production have altered the natural balances that have sustained life for millions of years. The unchecked

pursuit of development has often overlooked long-term consequences, leading to a growing gap between our needs and the planet's capacity to meet them sustainably.
Air, water, and soil pollution threaten human health and biodiversity, while the destruction of natural habitats accelerates species loss and ecosystem degradation. It is time to recognize the responsibility of our actions and actively engage in seeking solutions that restore balance.

Need for Change and Adoption of Sustainable Practices

The current situation demands deep reflection and decisive action. The need for change is undeniable, and the adoption of sustainable practices emerges as the key to reversing the course. Transitioning to renewable energy sources, reducing the use of non-recyclable materials, promoting energy efficiency, and environmental awareness are just some of the paths to pursue. Creating a global agenda that promotes the adoption of sustainable policies at governmental, corporate, and individual levels is imperative. Education and awareness are powerful tools in this battle, as community empowerment and collective awareness are key catalysts for change.

In this chapter, we explore the urgent challenge of addressing global environmental challenges, recognizing our impact, and embracing the need for change. We are called to become agents of change, to embrace sustainable practices, and to work together to preserve the beauty and diversity of our planet for future generations. Sustainability is not just an option; it is the necessary path to a future where our common home thrives and flourishes.

Chapter 4: Innovation as the Engine of Sustainability

At the heart of the transformation towards a sustainable future, innovation emerges as the driving force, capable of guiding us through a path of change and creating intelligent solutions for global environmental challenges. This chapter explores the crucial role of innovation in sustainable development, presents successful case studies of companies that have adopted sustainable innovations, and takes a fascinating look at emerging technologies that promise to shape a greener future.

Role of Innovation in Sustainable Development

Innovation is the key that unlocks new horizons in the context of sustainability. It goes beyond the creation of new products or services, embracing an approach that redefines entire systems and ways of operating. Sustainable innovation involves the constant search for solutions that not only address immediate problems but also contribute to building a resiliently sustainable future. The adoption of innovative practices and technologies is essential to reduce the environmental impact of human activities. From renewable energies to sustainable agricultural practices, from energy efficiency to waste management technologies, innovation manifests as a transformative force capable of guiding change towards a more sustainable society.

Case Studies of Companies Successfully Adopting Sustainable Innovations

Inspiration can arise from examples, and numerous business pioneers are demonstrating that sustainable innovation is not only possible but also profitable. Through in-depth case studies, we will examine the strategies adopted by leading companies in the field of sustainability. From technology companies incorporating the use of recycled materials into their products to agricultural organizations embracing sustainable farming practices, we will explore the challenges faced, the solutions adopted, and the positive impacts generated by these initiatives. These concrete examples demonstrate that sustainable innovation is not only a moral imperative but also a competitive advantage for forward-thinking companies.

Emerging Technologies to Address Environmental Challenges

Looking to the future, we explore emerging technologies that emerge as key tools in the fight against environmental challenges. From carbon capture and storage technologies to artificial intelligence-based solutions for sustainable resource management, innovation continues to push the boundaries. The connection between the Internet of Things (IoT) and sustainability offers surprising possibilities for more efficient monitoring and control of resources, while clean energy technologies pave the way for a future where our dependence on fossil fuels can be replaced by sustainable and renewable energy sources.

This chapter is an invitation to explore the extraordinary potential of innovation, both through the experiences of visionary companies that have embraced sustainability and through a forward-looking perspective on emerging technologies that will shape our path towards a greener and more prosperous world. In a

world driven by sustainable
innovation, change is inevitable,
and opportunities are limitless.

Chapter 5: Design Thinking and Sustainability

In an increasingly complex world, the synergy between design thinking and sustainability reveals itself as a powerful alchemy capable of shaping innovative and sustainable solutions that address global challenges. This chapter ventures into the creative territory of design thinking, exploring how this methodology can be applied to develop sustainable solutions. Through user-centered design and a focus on environmental impact, we will discover tangible examples of successful projects that embody the fusion of creativity and sustainability.

Application of Design Thinking to Develop Sustainable Solutions

Design thinking is a methodology that places the user at the center of the creative process, pushing towards solutions that truly respond to people's needs and aspirations. When applied to sustainability, it becomes a powerful tool for developing innovative solutions that not only meet user needs but also respect the environment. We explore how the iterative process of design thinking—understand, observe, ideate, prototype, and test—can be adapted to address complex environmental challenges. The human-centered approach enables the identification of more effective and acceptable approaches, considering people's needs alongside ecosystem impacts.

User-Centered Design and Environmental Impact

User-centered design is a cornerstone of design thinking and becomes even more relevant when discussing sustainability. The goal is not only to create environmentally friendly products or services but also to ensure that these respond to user needs in a practical and aesthetically pleasing way. Sustainability becomes an integral part of the user experience, encouraging conscious choices and responsible behaviors. We tackle the challenge of reconciling user-centered design with an environmentally sustainable approach. How can we create desirable, functional, and ecological products? This chapter explores methodologies and strategies that allow for balancing these needs, demonstrating that sustainability can enhance the user experience rather than limit it.

Examples of Successful Projects Based on Design Thinking

Theory comes to life through tangible examples of successful projects that embody the philosophy of design thinking applied to sustainability. From innovative packaging solutions to sustainable mobility services, these projects demonstrate that creativity and sustainability can go hand in hand, generating positive impacts on a broad scale. We explore the journey of projects that have addressed complex challenges, overcoming obstacles through the design thinking approach. Each example offers valuable insights into how user-centered innovation can drive change towards a more sustainable world.

In this chapter, we delve into the power of design thinking, discovering how this methodology can be a guiding beacon for creating sustainable solutions that enhance people's lives without compromising the well-being of our planet. Sustainability thus becomes not only a matter of necessity but of beauty and creative intuition.

Chapter 6: Sustainability in Industry and Business

In the context of a constantly evolving global economy, the role of businesses in sustainable innovation has become crucial in shaping a balanced and environmentally respectful future. This chapter explores the profound connection between sustainability, industry, and businesses, examining the key role organizations play in driving sustainable innovation. Through a deep dive into sustainable business practices and the examination of low-impact business models, we will unveil how companies can become agents of positive change in the fight against environmental challenges.

Role of Businesses in Sustainable Innovation

As engines of the global economy, businesses play a crucial role in sustainable innovation. The adoption of responsible business practices not only impacts the direct environmental footprint of operations but can also inspire systemic changes at an industrial level. Businesses can become pioneers, challenging the status quo and demonstrating that sustainability is not only ethical but also profitable. We examine how companies, through their ability to invest in research and development, can promote sustainable innovation not only within their own operations but throughout the entire supply chain. From the development of new eco-friendly materials to the implementation of low-impact production processes, the role of businesses is crucial in directing innovation towards a more sustainable path.

Sustainable Business Practices

Sustainable business practices go beyond mere compliance with environmental regulations. They involve a comprehensive review of operations, supply chains, and corporate policies to reduce the negative impact on the environment. From waste recycling to carbon emissions reduction, from corporate social responsibility (CSR) policies to the adoption of certified standards, businesses can embrace a systemic approach that integrates sustainability into every aspect of their activities. We examine real-life examples of companies that have successfully implemented sustainable business practices, highlighting the challenges faced and the benefits generated. These examples demonstrate that sustainability is not just a matter of image but a forward-thinking business strategy that can lead to long-term competitive advantages.

Low-Impact Environmental Business Models

In pursuit of sustainable innovation, businesses are increasingly adopting low-impact environmental business models. From transitioning to circular models that promote reuse and recycling to responsible production practices that minimize waste, these models demonstrate that it is possible to thrive economically while reducing environmental impact. We explore the characteristics of low-impact environmental business models, showcasing companies that have successfully embraced this approach. The transition to a circular economy and the redefinition of value chains become key strategies for addressing environmental challenges in a sustainable manner.

This chapter invites businesses to explore their crucial role in sustainable innovation, recognizing that the adoption of sustainable business practices and the creation of low-impact environmental business models are fundamental to building a prosperous and environmentally respectful future.

Chapter 7: Green and Renewable Technologies

In the journey towards a sustainable future, green and renewable technologies emerge as the protagonists of an energy revolution that can reshape how we live and operate. This chapter explores the fundamental role of renewable energy as a pillar of sustainable innovation, examining recent developments in green technologies and revealing the importance of sustainable energy in urban and industrial contexts.

Renewable Energy as a Pillar of Sustainable Innovation

Renewable energy is the beating heart of sustainable innovation, representing a crucial step towards reducing the environmental impact of traditional energy sources. This section of the book examines how green technologies are redefining the energy sector, promoting a transition to clean, efficient, and low-impact energy sources. From solar to wind, hydropower to geothermal, we explore different renewable energy sources and their potential in shaping a sustainable future. Through insights into energy storage technologies and smart grids, we discover how renewable energy not only reduces greenhouse gas emissions but also contributes to greater resilience and energy autonomy.

Recent Developments in Green Technologies

The landscape of green technologies is constantly evolving, with innovations opening new horizons in energy production, distribution, and utilization. We examine the latest developments in key sectors such as energy storage, high-efficiency solar cells, advanced wind turbines, and carbon capture and storage technologies. The integration of artificial intelligence, the Internet of Things (IoT), and innovative materials is redefining the landscape of green technologies, enabling more efficient and sustainable use of resources. Through case studies and practical examples, we explore how these new technologies are shaping our transition to a society based on sustainable energy.

Sustainable Energy in Urban and Industrial Contexts

The growing urbanization and continuous industrial development pose unique challenges that require innovative energy solutions. This chapter explores how sustainable energy fits into the urban and industrial context, outlining the challenges and opportunities that arise in these environments. From implementing zero-energy buildings and smart energy grids in cities to adopting low-impact production processes in industries, we analyze how green technologies can radically transform our daily lives and the way we produce goods and services. Through examples of innovative urban projects and sustainable industrial initiatives, we explore pathways for a global and inclusive energy transition.

This chapter guides us through renewable energy as the driving force of sustainable innovation, demonstrating how green technologies are not only the key to reducing environmental impact but also catalysts for a future where energy is a positive force for our society and our planet.

Chapter 8: Sustainable Mobility

In an ever-evolving world, sustainable mobility emerges as the engine of a crucial change, challenging traditional transportation paradigms and paving the way for a future where moving around is not only efficient but also environmentally friendly. This chapter explores the realm of sustainable mobility, highlighting low-impact transportation, electric vehicles, and smart mobility solutions, analyzing the impact of this revolution on urban and environmental configurations.

Low-Impact Environmental Transportation

Traditional transportation often represents one of the main sources of polluting emissions. However, sustainable mobility aims to transform this landscape by introducing low-impact transportation. We explore innovative solutions such as electric vehicles, electric bicycles, shared scooters, and efficient, clean public transportation. The reduction of greenhouse gas emissions, the decrease in air pollution, and the creation of healthier urban environments are just a few of the benefits resulting from this transition to low-impact transportation. Through case studies and concrete examples, we discover how cities worldwide are embracing this revolution, promoting more sustainable and accessible modes of transportation.

Electric Vehicles and Smart Mobility Solutions

Electric vehicles are a cornerstone of sustainable mobility, offering an eco-friendly and efficient alternative to traditional internal combustion engine vehicles. We examine recent developments in electric vehicles, from the increasing battery range to the widespread availability of charging infrastructure. Smart mobility, supported by technologies like artificial intelligence and the Internet of Things (IoT), is redefining the user experience and promoting more efficient and shared use of transportation. We explore how smart mobility solutions, such as car-sharing services and ride-sharing platforms, contribute to reducing the number of vehicles on the road while optimizing travel and reducing overall environmental impact. Through practical examples, we see how these solutions are changing how we move and interact with urban mobility.

Impact of Sustainable Mobility on Cities

Sustainable mobility is not just about vehicles; it has a profound impact on the structure and development of cities. We examine how the promotion of low-impact environmental transportation and smart mobility solutions influences urban planning, air quality, and the livability of cities. The creation of restricted traffic zones, the promotion of bike lanes, and the facilitation of efficient public transportation are just some of the strategies that cities are adopting to embrace sustainable mobility. We analyze the outcomes of these initiatives, exploring how cities are becoming more sustainable, inclusive, and geared towards the well-being of their residents.

This chapter provides an in-depth look at sustainable mobility, demonstrating how the adoption of low-impact environmental transportation and smart mobility solutions is shaping a future where travel is not only more efficient but also environmentally respectful. Sustainable mobility is not just a change in vehicles but a radical transformation of our conception of urban space and the possibilities for sustainable connection.

Chapter 9: Social and Community Innovation

At the heart of the transformation towards a more sustainable world, social and community innovation emerges as the pivot of initiatives that go beyond technology, engaging people and communities in shaping a fair and environmentally respectful future. This chapter explores grassroots initiatives at the local level, projects involving the community in sustainability, and the importance of community empowerment.

Grassroots Initiatives at the Local Level

Grassroots initiatives at the local level represent the beating heart of social and community innovation. We examine how communities are addressing specific challenges, creating unique solutions adaptable to the local context. From urban agriculture to local energy cooperatives, we explore how these initiatives contribute to strengthening social fabric and promoting neighborhood-level sustainability. Through practical examples, we see how grassroots projects, often born from collaboration between citizens and local organizations, can become driving forces for change. These initiatives demonstrate that sustainability is not just a global concept but manifests in concrete actions at the local level that respond to the specific needs of communities.

Projects Involving the Community in Sustainability

Active community involvement is essential for the success of sustainable initiatives. We examine projects that not only bring environmental benefits but actively engage residents, making them feel an integral part of the decision-making process and the creation of sustainable solutions. From awareness campaigns on waste separation to community-managed reforestation initiatives, we discover how collective action can generate significant impacts. Through success stories, we explore how community engagement projects can create a sense of belonging and responsibility, promoting sustainability as a shared lifestyle. These projects demonstrate that social innovation is a catalyst for change when the community is at the center of the process.

The Importance of Community Empowerment

Community empowerment is the key to ensuring that sustainable initiatives have a lasting impact. We examine how empowerment can be integrated into social innovation initiatives, enabling communities to acquire the skills and resources needed to lead their sustainable development. Through training programs, mentorship, and active participation in project planning and implementation, communities can become active agents in creating their future. We analyze cases where community empowerment has led to tangible results, showing that when people are provided with the right tools, they become the true guardians of sustainability.

In this chapter, we explore social and community innovation as a driving force towards a fairer and more sustainable world. From grassroots initiatives to community collaborations, we highlight how positive change can arise from every corner of society, giving voice to individuals and communities in shaping a more inclusive and environmentally respectful future.

Chapter 10: Challenges and Future Perspectives

In our journey towards a sustainable future, understanding the persistent challenges that still hinder the complete adoption of sustainable innovations is crucial. This chapter explores these challenges, analyzing future trends and developments in sustainability while emphasizing the fundamental role of education and awareness in promoting sustainable innovation.

Persistent Challenges in Adopting Sustainable Innovations

Despite extraordinary progress in sustainable innovation, there are persistent challenges that require creative solutions and collective commitments. We examine the economic, social, and cultural barriers limiting the adoption of sustainable practices. From resistance to change to disparities in access, we understand how these challenges can compromise efforts towards a more sustainable society. Through in-depth analysis, we explore how public policies, private sector engagement, and social activism can effectively address these challenges. Seeking solutions to persistent challenges is essential to ensure that sustainable innovation becomes a distinctive feature of our society.

Future Trends and Developments in Sustainability

Looking to the future, we examine key trends and developments that will shape the sustainability landscape. From new technologies to circular economy strategies, we explore how innovation will continue to evolve to address emerging environmental challenges. Case studies and projections immerse us in future scenarios, offering a clear vision of the potentials and challenges that lie ahead. Analyzing future trends allows us to anticipate opportunities and prepare for upcoming challenges. We explore how adapting to new realities, flexibility, and cross-sector collaboration can be key to success in promoting sustainability globally.

Role of Education and Awareness in Promoting Sustainable Innovation

Education and awareness emerge as the foundations upon which the long-term sustainability is built. We examine the crucial role of education in shaping informed citizens capable of understanding and appreciating the importance of sustainable innovation. Through targeted educational programs, both formal and informal, we explore how we can cultivate a new generation of mindful leaders and conscious consumers.

Public awareness is essential to support significant political and behavioral changes. We analyze how awareness campaigns, media, and civil society initiatives can contribute to building widespread awareness of the need to adopt sustainable practices. Awareness is the first step towards action, and active public engagement is crucial to fuel the drive towards sustainable innovation.

In conclusion, this chapter offers a comprehensive perspective on current and future challenges surrounding sustainable innovation. Through the analysis of trends, exploration of persistent challenges, and emphasis on the critical role of education and awareness, we prepare for a future where sustainable innovation is not just a goal but an integrated reality in our society and lives.

Chapter 11: Conclusions

In this compelling journey through sustainable innovation, we arrive at the conclusions, where we reflect on the key concepts that have emerged and issue a call to action and global collaboration. We conclude by exploring the vision of a sustainable and resilient future, driven by the enthusiasm for positive change.

Summary of Key Concepts

Our journey through the preceding chapters has led us to explore the multiple dimensions of sustainable innovation. We have defined the concept, examined the foundations of sustainability, and analyzed challenges and opportunities in different sectors. We've explored the crucial roles of communities, businesses, and green technologies in shaping a sustainable future. In this summary phase, we revisit key concepts: the importance of sustainability in every sector of society, innovation as a driver of change, and the urgent need to adopt more sustainable practices to preserve our planet.

Call to Action and Global Collaboration

The challenge of sustainable innovation is a shared commitment for all of us. We issue a passionate call to action and global collaboration. Every individual, every community, every business has a crucial role to play. It is time to move from awareness to action, to make responsible decisions, and to promote sustainability in every aspect of our lives. Global collaboration is the key to addressing environmental challenges on a large scale. Collective efforts, sharing best practices, and cooperation between nations can accelerate the transition to a sustainable future. Our call is an open invitation to all who share the vision of a better world and are ready to contribute actively.

Vision of a Sustainable and Resilient Future

We conclude with an inspiring vision of a sustainable and resilient future. We imagine a world where renewable energies power our cities, zero-emission transports traverse the streets, and communities thrive through sustainable practices. A future where nature is respected and preserved, and social equity is at the core of every decision. Resilience characterizes this future, with communities and ecosystems capable of facing challenges with flexibility and solidarity. The constant pursuit of sustainable innovation is the engine of this future, guiding humanity toward conscious and responsible choices.

In this vision, each of us is an agent of change, contributing to a world where sustainability is not just a goal but an everyday reality. Our conclusion is an invitation to look forward with hope and commitment, ready to build together a sustainable and promising future for generations to come.

Appendix: Useful Resources

Sustainable innovation is a vast field nourished by knowledge, inspiration, and best practices from multiple sources. This appendix provides a comprehensive list of useful resources, including organizations committed to sustainability, enlightening books, captivating documentaries, and informative websites. Delving into these resources is an excellent way to expand one's understanding of sustainable innovation and embark on a deeper journey toward a greener future.

Organizations

- **World Green Building Council (WGBC):**
- WGBC is an international organization promoting sustainability in the

construction industry, leading the sector toward greener and healthier buildings.

- **Sustainable Apparel Coalition (SAC):**

- SAC brings together companies in the apparel industry to promote sustainable and transparent practices throughout the production chain.

- **Ellen MacArthur Foundation:**

- The Ellen MacArthur Foundation is committed to the circular economy, advocating for repair, reuse, and recycling as key elements of sustainability.

- **World Resources Institute (WRI):**

- WRI is a global research organization dedicated to sustainable solutions for environmental challenges such as climate change and biodiversity loss.

Books

- **"Cradle to Cradle: Remaking the Way We Make Things" by William McDonough and Michael Braungart:**

- This book proposes a revolutionary approach to design, emphasizing the creation of products that can be fully recycled or composted.

- **"The Upcycle: Beyond Sustainability—Designing for Abundance" by William McDonough and Michael Braungart:**

- A sequel to the previous book, exploring how upcycling can lead to even more sustainable solutions.

- **"Drawdown: The Most Comprehensive Plan Ever Proposed to Reverse Global Warming" by Paul Hawken:**

- Hawken presents a detailed plan with concrete solutions to reverse global warming.

- **"Doughnut Economics: Seven Ways to Think Like a 21st-Century Economist" by Kate Raworth:**

- Raworth challenges the traditional economic model and proposes a circular and sustainable approach based on "doughnut economics."

Documentaries

- **"Before the Flood" - Leonardo DiCaprio:**

- This documentary follows Leonardo DiCaprio as he explores the impacts of climate change and possible solutions.

- **"Our Planet" - Narrated by Sir David Attenborough:**

- A documentary series that explores the beauty of nature and highlights the environmental threats our planet faces.

- **"Minimalism: A Documentary About the Important Things":**

- This documentary explores minimalism as a sustainable lifestyle, encouraging a reduction in consumption and a focus on meaningful things.

Websites

- **GreenBiz:**
- GreenBiz provides news, resources, and analysis on sustainable practices in the business world.

- **Sustainable Brands:**
- A platform connecting businesses and professionals committed to building sustainable and responsible brands.

- **The Guardian - Environment Section:**
- A reliable source of environmental news,

reports, and analysis to stay informed about the latest developments in sustainability.

Exploring these resources will provide a broad spectrum of information and inspiration for anyone looking to deepen their understanding of sustainable innovation and actively contribute to building a better future for our planet.

Printed in Great Britain
by Amazon